THE BENEFITS OF THE SPEAKING FAITH

Abraham believed when he stood in the presence of the God who gives life to dead people and calls into existence things that don't even exist.

Romans 4:17 *God's word translation*

by
Franklin N. Abazie

The Benefits of the Speaking Faith
COPYRIGHT @ 2016 by Franklin N. Abazie
ISBN: 978-1-94513318-3

All right reserved. This book or any portion thereof may not be reproduced or used in any manner whatsoever without the express written permission of the publisher, except for the use of brief quotations in a book review. All Bible quotes are from King James Version and others as noted.

Published by: F N ABAZIE PUBLISHING HOUSE—
a.k.a. Empowerment Bookstore

*That I may publish with the voice of thanksgiving
and tell of all thy wondrous works.*
Psalm 26:7

To order additional copies, wholesales or booking call:
the Church office (973.372.7518)
or Empowerment Bookstore Hotline (973.393.8518)

Worship address:
343 Sanford Avenue, Newark, New Jersey 07106
Administrative Head Office address:
33 Schley Street Newark New Jersey 07112
Email: pastorfranknto@yahoo.com
Website www.fnabaziehealingministries.org
Publishing House: www.fnabaziepublishinghouse.org

This book is a production of F N Abazie Publishing House. A publication Arms of Miracle of God Ministries 2016.
First Edition

CONTENTS

THE MANDATE OF THE COMMISSION....................iv
ARMS OF THE COMMISSION...................................v
INTRODUCTION..vi

CHAPTER 1
The Power of the Spoken Word.................................1

CHAPTER 2
The Mystery of the Right Word...............................13

CHAPTER 3
The Laws of Speaking Faith....................................22

CHAPTER 4
Prayer of Salvation...59
About the Author..66

THE MANDATE OF THE COMMISSION

"The moment is due to impact your world through the revival of the healing & miracle ministry of Jesus Christ of Nazareth.

"I am sending you to restore health unto thee and I will heal thee of thy wounds, said the Lord of Host."

ARMS OF THE COMMISSION

1) F N Abazie Ministries—Miracle of God Ministries (Miracle Chapel Intl)

2) F N Abazie TV Ministries: Global Television Ministry Outreach

3) F N Abazie Radio Ministries: Radio Broadcasting Outreach

4) F N Abazie Publishing House: Book Publication

5) F N Abazie Bible School: also called Word of Healing Bible School (W.O.H.B.S.)

6) F N Abazie Evangelistic Ass: Miracle of God Ministries: Global Crusade

7) Empowerment Bookstore: Book distribution

8) F N Abazie Helping Hands: Meeting the Help of the Needy Worldwide

9) F N Abazie Disaster Recovery Mission: Global Disaster Recovery

10) F N Abazie Prison Ministry: Prison Ministry For All Convicts "Second Chance"

Some of our ministry arms are awaiting the appointed time to commence.

INTRODUCTION

In my opinion, FAITH is a KINGDOM mystery that comes with revelation beyond our human explanation. Although there is no idle word in the kingdom of GOD, most of us BELIEVERS have NEGLECTED and IGNORED the POWER of the SPOKEN WORD. JESUS made it clear to us—there is no idle WORD in the KINGDOM of GOD. Oftentimes, most of us carelessly speak negative words into the atmosphere, which continues to POLICE our lives and HINDERS us from fulfilling our calling in Christ Jesus. (DESTINY). The Bible says, therefore whatsoever you desire when you pray, *"believe that ye receive them and ye shall have them."* (Mark 11:24)

As a young man growing up, I underestimated the power of God on my tongue through the mystery of faith. In my own understanding—"faith is no cheap talk." A talk of faith is a talk of triumph and victory in life.

For it is God who is working in you, enabling you both to desire and to work out His good purpose.
Philippians 2:13

In our lifetime, there is nothing we—believers and non-believers—can accomplish in life without the

POWER OF FAITH. Although we have not taken this into account, we do almost everything in life by FAITH.

FAITH IS THE POWER OF LIFE

As thou knowest not what is the way of the spirit,
how the bones do grow in the womb of her
that is with child: even so thou knowest
not the works of God who maketh all.
Ecclesiastes 11:5

We all must live and operate by FAITH, otherwise we lose our inheritance in GOD. A lot of us have so much contradicted the WORD OF GOD that, the REVELATION and MYSTERY of FAITH has lost its ROOT value. Faith in my own understanding is a shield for our DELIVERANCE, a BREAKTHROUGH plat form against all trial and tribulations of life.

FAITH IS A SHIELD FOR OUR DEFENCE

Above all, taking the shield of faith, wherewith ye shall
be able to quench all the fiery darts of the wicked.
Ephesians 6:16

With the shield of FAITH, we are protected against the devil's wiles and schemes. As long as we speak faith into our circumstances, the devil has no chance to prevail against our lives. It takes the mystery of faith to understand the revelation of "greater is he that is in you, than he that is in the world."

FAITH IS OUR VICTORY CERTIFICATION

For whatsoever is born of God overcometh the world: and this is the victory that overcometh the world, even our faith.
1 John 5:4

We do not stand a chance to prevail against any life challenges and obstacles, unless FAITH takes its perspective in our lives. FAITH is our VICTORY CERTIFICATION against all the brutal attacks of the devil. It is the mystery of faith that will subdue and overcome the wicked one (the devil).

WE WALK IN LIFE BY FAITH

For we walk by faith, not by sight.
2 Corinthians 5:7

For destinies to be fulflied in life, we must walk by faith. No one will go far in life without the help of faith. The Bible says, *"But without faith it is impossible to please him: for he that cometh to God must believe that he is, and that he is a rewarder of them that diligently seek him."* (Hebrews 11:6) As long as we desire to please GOD in life, we must therefore walk by faith.

WE STAND BY FAITH

Not for that we have dominion over your faith, but are helpers of: your joy: for by faith ye stand.
2 Corinthians 1:24

It takes FAITH to withstand opposition forces. *"Wherefore take unto you the whole armour of God that ye may be able to withstand in the evil day, and having done all, to stand. Stand therefore, having your loins girt about with truth, and having on the breastplate of righteousness."* (Ephesians 6:13-14)

*For we wrestle not against flesh and blood,
but against principalities, against powers,
against the rulers of the darkness of this world,
against spiritual wickedness in high places.*
Ephesians 6:12

In these evil days, OUR SECURED VICTORY against the challenges of life must be established by FAITH. Although FAITH works by LOVE, our works must be proven by our faith in GOD...

So faith without works is dead also. It is my desire in this book for your life to be transformed by faith. Feel free to pray in faith even as you read this book.

HAPPY READING!

HIGHLIGHTS ON FAITH

WHAT IS FAITH?

Hebrews 11:1 gives us a unique definition of faith. "Now faith is the substance of things hoped for, the evidence of things not seen." Faith is believing GOD that it shall be well, in the midst of frustration. Faith means looking up to GOD with a positive mindset, that it will get better.

So many of us does not have the conviction of faith. It is the conviction that brings the cure. *"And blessed is she that believed: for there shall be a performance of those things which were told her from the Lord."* The centurion in Matthew 8:8 said, *"But speak the word only, and my servant shall be healed. As long as there is no convicted, it is not Faith."*

HOW DOES FAITH COME?

Bible recorded that FAITH comes by HEARING. Romans10:17 So then faith cometh by hearing, and hearing by the word of God. WE ARE ADMOINSHED BY SCRIPTURE TO BUILD UP OUR SELVES IN OUR MOST HOLY FAITH BY PRAYING IN THE SPIRIT. Without praying in the SPIRIT we cannot BUILD UP OUR SELVES. Jude1:20 But ye beloved, building up your selves on your most holy faith, praying in the Holy Ghost.

HOW DOES FAITH WORK?

FAITH WORKS BY LOVE.

But faith which worketh by love.
Galatians 5:6

Faith is a KINGDOM mystery that works only by LOVE. As long as there is no LOVE inside of us, FAITH will not work. *Yea, a man may say, Thou hast faith, and I have works: shew me thy faith without thy works, and I will shew thee my faith by my works.* (James 2:18)

PRAYER POINT TO ACTIVATE THE POWER OF FAITH INSIDE OF US

1) Father Lord, empower me to develop faith, in the Name of Jesus.

2) Power of God, mightily magnify faith inside of me, in the Name of Jesus.

3) Blood of Jesus, break me through, in the Name of Jesus.

4) Heavenly Father, change my story, in the Name of Jesus.

5) Power of God, reverse my story for good, in the Name of Jesus.

6) Hand of God, destroy all my persecutors, in the Name of Jesus.

7) Fire of God, roast all hindering spirit prevailing over my glorious destiny.

8) I established jurisdiction over all my given real estate territories, in the Name of Jesus.

9) Every power causing me to retain in frustration and despression, loosen your hold, in the Name of Jesus.

10) Father god break the strong hold of sin over my life in the Name of Jesus.

11) Lord God, emphasize genuine repentance over my Spirit man, in the Name of Jesus.

12) Holy Spirit, revive and rekindle your fire of revival inside of me, in the Name of Jesus.

13) Power of God, hijack the controlling forces oppressing my life, in the Name of Jesus.

14) I destroy all forces causing me to sin, in the Name of Jesus.

15) Blood of Jesus, take over my life, in the Name of Jesus.

16) O Lord, baptize me with the gift of the Holy Spirit.

17) Holy Spirit, breathe afresh upon my life in the Name of Jesus.

18) Holy Spirit, take possession of my will, in the Name of Jesus.

19) Holy Spirit, make yourself real to me, in the Name of Jesus

20) Holy Spirit, fan your revival fire upon my life, in the Name of Jesus

CHAPTER 1
THE POWER OF THE SPOKEN WORD

Is not my word like as a fire? saith the Lord; and like a hammer that breaketh the rock in pieces
JEREMIAH 23:29

In life the words we speak daily is as POWERFUL AS EVERY THING WE SEE. The bible says that the word of GOD is creative, prophetic, destructive, and medicinal. In the school of faith, what we say is what we get.

A man's belly shall be satisfied with the fruit of his mouth; and with the increase of his lips shall he be filled. Death and life are in the power of the tongue: and they that love it shall eat the fruit thereof.
Proverbs 18:20-21

After numerous experiences in life, I concluded that there is an inexplicable supernatural power in the word we speak daily.

"What you say is what you will get."

For verily I say unto you, That whosoever shall say unto this mountain, Be thou removed, and be thou cast into the sea; and shall not doubt in his heart, but shall believe that those things which he saith shall come to pass; he shall have whatsoever he saith.
Mark 11:23

As believers, every word we speak carries a SUPERNATURAL POWER FROM GOD. It proceeds with a force because it comes from the SPIRIT OF GOD IN US. We should always speak out in FAITH if we desire to see ANYTHING GOOD come to pass in our lifetime. *The words that I speak unto you, they are spirit, and they are life.* (John 6:63) We must be committed and responsible for every word we speak at all times.

Every powerful spoken word must be mixed with OUR FAITH.

What is faith?

Hebrews 11:1 puts it this way: *Now faith is the substance of things hoped for, the evidence of things not seen.* In my own definition, faith is a kingdom currency for all earthly transaction. Although we do almost everything in life by faith, we fail to apply faith in everything we engage ourselves in. *And he that doubteth is damned if he eat, because he eateth not of faith: for whatsoever is not of faith is sin.* (Romans 14:23)

Faith has a universal value—that is, it has the same unique potency worldwide. Oftentimes some of us think you can only apply faith in Africa, for example. I heard someone say, "You do not preach the gospel and get miracles in America, because the people over there have no faith." With faith you can get results anywhere it is applied. Jesus said to those two blind men in Matthew 9:29: *Then touched he their eyes, saying, According to your faith be it unto you.*

Faith is a kingdom mystery that has a concrete force to break any barrier. Faith has a superpower that commands and converts invincible things into tangible things. *And calleth those things which be not as though they were.* (Romans 4:17)

> *But I say unto you, That every idle word that men shall speak, they shall give account thereof in the day of judgment. For by thy words thou shalt be justified, and by thy words thou shalt be condemned.*
> **Matthew 12:36-37**

Words spoken out of the spirit of faith are creative. For faith takes the invincible words and converts them into visible things. (Those things that be not as if they are, when spoken from the realms of the spirit get converted.)

Faith has divine power, which I call supernatural forces; this force has the ability to create and to destroy, to build and to plant; to throw down and to manifest known objects and unknown inanimate objects in the earthly realm. Faith has power to convert spoken word into money. Jesus delegated Peter to get money from the mouth of a fish. The fish heard Jesus and responded. *Notwithstanding, lest we should offend them, go thou to the sea, and cast an hook, and take up the fish that first cometh up; and when thou hast opened his mouth, thou shalt find a piece of money: that take, and give unto them for me and thee.* (Matthew 17:27)

> *We having the same spirit of faith,*
> *according as it is written, I believed,*
> *and therefore have I spoken; we also believe,*
> *and therefore speak*
> **2 Corinthians 4:13**

The power of the spoken words is activated only by the force of faith. Faith therefore is the platform to generate the RIGHT WORD, THE VICTORY WORD, THE HEALING WORD, etc. Jesus said there is no idle word in the kingdom. *But I say unto you, That every idle word that men shall speak, they shall give account thereof in the day of judgment. (*Matthew 12:36)

Unless we embrace the truth of the words we speak daily, we will always divert our blessing with our mouth. The words in your mouth will never command the positive result as long as you speak against yourselves. By this I mean—whatever you say is what you will see. *And the LORD said unto Moses, I will do this thing also that thou hast spoken.* (Exodus 33:17)

Every word spoken out of faith has a potent force, this force has creative genes to duplicate whatever command it receives. It has Power to lift and to cast down. The spoken words has power to create and authority to divert, and, stop any contrary force or evil forces against anyone. In the school of faith, we do not confess lack, we do not confess negative words, otherwise those negative words will manifest in our lives The Power of the spoken word is the primary source for unstoppable divine supply.

Who against hope believed in hope, that he might become the father of many nations, according to that which was spoken, So shall thy seed be.
And being not weak in faith, he considered not his own body now dead, when he was about an hundred years old, neither yet the deadness of Sarah's womb:
He staggered not at the promise of God through unbelief; but was strong in faith, giving glory to God; And being fully persuaded that, what he had promised, he was able also to perform.
Romans 4:18-21

The gift of faith will bring salvation unto you. *For by grace are ye saved through faith.* (Ephesians 2:8) While word of faith will give you knowledge, which I call information, it is the spirit of faith that will deliver the manifestation of our long-awaited blessing and promotions in life. As long as we are not right with GOD, we cannot speak anything into existence. Sin is the barrier that will hinder the spoken word from manifesting in our lives.

What is sin, one may ask?

One man said S.I.N means Satan Identification Number, I do not disagree, but it is incomplete. In my own definition, sin is disobeying God words and commandments. Every time you operate outside of the commandment of God you are committing sin. 1John3:8 He that committeth sin is of the devil; for the devil sinneth from the beginning. For this purpose the son of God was manifested that he might destroy the works of the devil.

> *Now we know that God heareth not sinners:*
> *but if any man be a worshipper of God,*
> *and doeth his will, him he heareth.*
> **John 9:31**

Sin is a force that will HINDER every spoken positive word in life. *For I acknowledge my transgressions and my sin is ever before me. (*Psalm 51:3) We all were born in sin, the Bible testified. *Behold I was shapen in iniquity; and in sin did my mother conceive me.* (Psalm 51:5) We are guarded by our conscience to discern do good, and not evil in life. We must all strive to make a mark for Jesus Christ by living RIGHT in our life time.

Who is a Sinner?

There is a POWER that pushes us all into any sinful lifestyle. Until such forces are crushed, it has power to prevail over the life of the believer. On the subject of who is a sinner, there is no exemption—everyone is included. It's time to tell yourself the truth. Is there any hidden sinful lifestyle you are dealing with? Confess it and crush it in the open with prayers.

Examine yourselves, whether ye be in the faith; prove your own selves. Know ye not your own selves, how that Jesus Christ is in you, except ye be reprobates?
2 Corinthians 13:5

Although most faith people live in denial about the work of the flesh, from my own scriptural understanding, everyone operating within the scope of Galatians 5:20-21 is classified as a sinner.

Now the works of the flesh are manifest, which are these; Adultery, fornication, uncleanness, lasciviousness, Idolatry, witchcraft, hatred, variance, emulations, wrath, strife, seditions, heresies, Envyings, murders, drunkenness, revellings, and such like: of the which I tell you before, as I have also told you in time past, that they which do such things shall not inherit the kingdom of God.
Galatians 5:20-21

Further supporting scripture....

But the fearful, and unbelieving, and the abominable, and murderers, and whoremongers, and sorcerers, and idolaters, and all liars, shall have their part in the lake which burneth with fire and brimstone: which is the second death.
Revelation 21:8

Who is therefore a sinner?

1) The Lazy Man: It is sinful for any able-bodied man or woman to fold their hands and make themselves beggars. The Bible says *"the sluggard will not plow by reason of the cold; therefore shall he beg in harvest, and have nothing."* (Proverbs 20:4) In my own understanding, laziness is a sin. *For even when we were with you, this we commanded you, that if any would not work, neither should he eat.* (2 Thessalonians 3:10) Covenant mentality demands that we all understand that God has done His part over our lives. Jesus said I must work. It is dignified for every believer to earn money through the work of their hands—although most lazy people live in denial and tend to blame someone else. Nevertheless, Godliness demands that we take absolute responsibility for the outcome of our lives.

2) Unbelievers: In my view, all that have not acknowledged Jesus Christ as Lord and savior are sinners. The Bible says *God heareth not sinners*. Without contradiction, all unbelievers live in a sinful lifestyle. Unless God has mercy, most unbelievers will not make eternity in heaven.

3) Liars: All liars are sinners before the Almighty God. Lying is a very serious sin, simply because it leads to poverty and shame. Lying decays great destiny and erodes potential future. Someone who I know very well lies so much to themselves, they became a beggar by paralyzing their future and frustrating the will of God over their life.

How do I come out of sin?

It takes a living force of faith to come out of sin. Apostle Paul said in Romans 7:23-25—*But I see another law in my members, warring against the law of my mind, and bringing me into captivity to the law of sin which is in my members. O wretched man that I am! who shall deliver me from the body of this death? I thank God through Jesus Christ our Lord. So then with the mind I myself serve the law of God; but with the flesh the law of sin. We must therefore be provoked by faith to come out of sin.*

You must *REPENT* & *CONFESS* & *PROCLAIM* THE LORD JESUS CHRIST

The word says as many as received him, to them gave He power to become the sons of God. Even to them that believe in his name. To qualify for divine visitation do the following (with sincerity):

1) ***Acknowledge*** that you are a sinner and that He died for you. (Romans 3:23)

2) ***Repent of your sins.*** (Acts 3:19, Luke 13:5, 2 Peter 3:9)

3) ***Believe in your heart*** that Jesus died for your sin.(Romans 10:10)

4) ***Confess Jesus as the Lord over your life.*** (Romans 10:10, Acts 2:21)

Now repeat this Prayer after me—

Say Lord Jesus, I accept you today, as my Lord and my savior, forgive me of my sins wash me with your blood. Right now, I believe, I am sanctified, I am save, I am free, I am free from the Power of sin to serve the Lord Jesus. Thank you Lord for saving me. Amen.

Congratulations.

YOU ARE NOW A BORN AGAIN CHRISTIAN!

STEPS TO OVERCOME THE LIFESTYLE OF SIN

YOU MUST BE BORN AGAIN

FAITH

FAITH is the living FORCE that will DELIVER US all from SIN. We must therefore BELIEVE in the FINISHED WORK OF JESUS CHRIST on the CROSS. Whenever FAITH steps into any life, there is always proof of transformation. *And be not conformed to this world: but be ye transformed by the renewing of your mind, that ye may prove what is that good, and acceptable, and perfect, will of God.* (Romans 12:2) Therefore, develop faith that will destroy all SINFUL HABITS IN YOUR LIFE.

PRAYER

We are admonished in the scripture that the only way to build up our faith is by PRAYING IN THE SPIIRT. Most of the relief and assurance that will come into our lives is on the platform of prayers. The significance of prayer cannot be overemphasized. PRAYER IS SO POWERFUL THAT IT WILL GIVE YOU HOPE. Most of us complain about challenges, but never create time to pray about it. We tell everybody about it, but we do not tell God about it. Every time we really talk to GOD in PRAYERS the devil knows.

HOW TO ACTIVATE THE HOLY SPIRIT IN YOUR LIFE

First of all, you must believe that there *is* a Holy Spirit.

1) *Acknowledge* the person of the Holy Spirt.

2) *Believe* in the ministration of the Holy Spirit

3) *Submit & obey* the person of the Holy Spirit.

4) *Welcome* the sweet presence of the Holy Spirit.

SUMMARY OF CHAPTER ONE

But I say unto you, That every idle word that men shall speak, they shall give account thereof in the day of judgment. For by thy words thou shalt be justified, and by thy words thou shalt be condemned.
Matthew 12:36

As simple as it sounds, we are responsible and accountable for every word we speak out in life.

We must be conscious of our daily utterance.

The words we speak daily are seed—if you add faith, it will fulfill its desire.

The POWER OF THE SPOKEN WORD MUST come out of FAITH.

CHAPTER 2
THE MYSTERY OF THE RIGHT WORD

And Peter calling to remembrance saith unto him, Master, behold, the fig tree which thou cursedst is withered away.
Mark 11:21

Every RIGHT word spoken out into the atmosphere in faith has tremendous POWER to MANIFEST and PREVAIL against all NEGATIVE WORDS, HINDERING our lives and destiny. Every RIGHT WORD and every PROPHETIC WORD SPOKEN IN FAITH HAS the backing of our Almighty GOD. We must all be cautious of the words we speak, especially in times of challenges and obstacles.

In Mark 11:21, Apostle Peter recalled Jesus cursing a fig tree and noticed the manifestation of the SPOKEN WORD of Jesus Christ the Master. *"The cursed fig tree obeyed the word of Jesus Christ and withered."*

With the accreditation of the blood of Jesus, and as spiritual law enforcement officers, we must enforce the laws of the SPIRIT by speaking out in faith ahead of the manifestation. In the laws of the spirit, "You get what you say." Whatever we decree, we believe we will get it and it comes to pass. T*herefore I say unto you, what things soever ye desire, when ye pray, believe that ye receive them, and ye shall have them.* (Mark 11:24) There is so much power in the spoken word. Jesus

Christ made it clear to us, there is no idle word in the kingdom of God.

> *But I say unto you, That every idle word that men shall speak, they shall give account thereof in the day of judgment.*
> **Matthew 12:36**

Although there is no idle word in the kingdom, we are responsible and accountable for every word that proceed out of our mouth. We must therefore speak the RIGHT word at all times.

> *For by thy words thou shalt be justified, and by thy words thou shalt be condemned.*
> **Matthew 12:37**

Every time we speak any word into the atmosphere casually, we become a casualty of our very word. Whenever we take for granted the words we speak, we become grounded by the same word.

Over the years, I have examined the words of a few folks around me. Those who concentrated on speaking the "RIGHT POSITIVE WORD" got their breakthroughs and succeeded in their endeavors. But those who spoke NEGATIVELY all the time with doubt and FEAR did not get breakthroughs—most of them are still in captivity and in bondage.

Although we easily forget unconsciously, we must enforce and see to it that we speak the "RIGHT" word at every prevailing circumstance.

> *How forcible are right words!*
> *but what doth your arguing reprove?*
> **Job 6:25**

It takes faith to enforce the RIGHT WORD all the time. Oftentimes we forget the backing of our great GOD "*where the word of a king is.*" *(*Ecclesiastes 8:4)

It takes the POWER OF PATIENCE to speak the RIGHT WORD in times of distress and calamity. Your patience to the spoken word is an indication that GOD's word is working.

> *My brethren, count it all joy when ye fall*
> *into divers temptations; Knowing this, that the*
> *trying of your faith worketh patience. But let*
> *patience have her perfect work, that ye may be*
> *perfect and entire, wanting nothing.*
> **James 1:2-4**

Note that the manifestation of the spoken word is effective if only we can endure temptation. The spoken RIGHT WORD in faith may be delayed, but eventually it will be fulfilled.

Every SPOKEN RIGHT WORD in faith is GOD'S WORD. And GOD'S WORD is GOD'S METHOD, And God's method needs FAITH, PATIENCE and ENDURANCE. God is never in a rush to change our story.

Recall with me that **God's words do not return void, but they accomplish what we desire and achieve the purpose for which we sent them**. *He that believeth shall not make haste.* (Isaiah 28:16) In Proverbs 28:20 the word says, *"He that maketh haste to be rich shall not be innocent."*

So shall my word be that goeth forth out of my mouth: it shall not return unto me void, but it shall accomplish that which I please, and it shall prosper in the thing whereto I sent it.
Isaiah 55:11

WHAT IS THE RIGHT WORD?

The RIGHT WORD is the word IN SEASON, the required word at the moment against the prevailing obstacle. *Is not my word like as a fire? saith the Lord; and like a hammer that breaketh the rock in pieces.* (Jeremiah 23:29) *I will make my words in thy mouth fire, and this people wood, and it shall devour them.* (Jeremiah 5:19)

He sent his word, and healed them, and delivered them from their destructions.
Psalm 107:20

THE RIGHT WORD
IS THE WORD OF DELIVERANCE

Every time you find yourself in any form of captivity, SPEAK THE RIGHT WORD OF FAITH in to the PREVAILING CIRCUMSTANCE.

THE RIGHT WORD
IS THE WORD OF HEALING

We are commanded by scripture to SPEAK THE RIGHT WORD OF HEALING AND WE SHALL BE HEALED. *But speak the word only, and my servant shall be healed.* (Matthew 8:8)

THE RIGHT WORD
IS THE WORD IN SEASON

There is a season for you. We must understand our SEASON OF CHALLENGE and our SEASON OF EASE. We must therefore speak THE RIGHT WORD in season. *The Lord God hath given me the tongue of the learned, that I should know how to speak a word in season to him that is weary.* (Isaiah 50:4)

GOD always tries and tests us to see if we are prepared and ready for the manifestation of THE SPOKEN RIGHT WORD. As long as we can endure trial and temptation, GOD will see us through in life. *Blessed is the man that endureth temptation: for when he is tried, he shall receive the crown of life, which the Lord hath promised to them that love him.* (James 1:12)

The story of Joseph in the scriptures painted a graphic picture of the POWER, MYSTERY & REWARD OF THE RIGHT WORD. The book of Genesis narrated that Joseph began his life with trials from his brothers at home. He became a slave in Egypt before emerging as a Deputy Governor to Pharaoh King of Egypt—until the time that his word came. The word of the Lord tried him.

In this end time we live in, we are not ready for the trials—but we want the triumph and the trophy. Reality theology teaches us that we must set attainable and realizable goals for our lives and future.

> *Neither shall they say, Lo here! or, lo there!*
> *for, behold, the kingdom of God is within you.*
> **Luke 17:21**

What we are preaching is that GOD is not a magician. The above scripture tells us that, *"the KINGDOM OF GOD IS WITHIN US."* Although most of us expect GOD to suddenly emerge—which is very true— there are still principles upon which we can provoke our desired miracles.

Every time you take the RIGHT STEP and SPEAK THE RIGHT WORD, you have committed GOD into that issue. Colin Powell once said, "A dream doesn't become reality through magic; it takes sweat, determination and hard work. Success is the result of perfection, hard work, learning from failure, loyalty, and persistence. There are no secrets to success. It is the result of preparation, hard work and learning from failure. If you are going to achieve excellence in big things, you develop the habit in little matters. Excellence is not an exception, it is a prevailing attitude."

Chapter 2   The Mystery of the Right Word

DECISION KEYS

1) Nothing changes until you make up your mind.

2) Decision is the gateway to deliverance.

3) Until you decide, no one will decide for you.

4) Your prosperity is proportional to your decisions.

5) The decision you make will determine the future you will create

6) Decision creates future and fulfills destinies.

7) Decision beautifies our future.

8) Decision keeps you out of trouble.

9) Decision exempts you from evil.

10) Decision gurantees eternity.

11) You can only go far in life by your faith decisions.

12) You are poor because you made such decisions

13) Make a decision and change your life.

14) Life changing decisions are a function of quality

information.

15) Success in life is a function of decision.

16) Life experiences are full of decisions.

17) Decisions change destinies.

18) Never settle for information—always look for revelation.

19) You are where you are today based on your last decision.

20) Information is crucial in decision making.

21) Decision makers rule the world.

22) You can rule your world with quality decisions.

23) As long as you decide rightly, Satan cannot harrass you.

CHAPTER 3
THE LAWS OF SPEAKING IN FAITH

Now faith is the substance of things hoped for, the evidence of things not seen.
Hebrews 11:1

WHAT IS FAITH?

Faith is the substance of things hoped for, the evidence of things not seen. Faith means activating the supernatural—the unseen—yet still believing in it. Faith ENCOURAGES us to be CONVINCED about the unseen and invisible and believe it—to act on it. FAITH is from God and FEAR is from Satan.

While FEAR provokes us to establish worry, fear, doubt and unbelief in our heart, FAITH ELIMINATES THOSE NEGETIVE WORDS. Faith replaces them with strength, wisdom, power, blessings, joy, happiness. Faith is a language of life in the SPIRIT. The word of God says, *Death and life are in the power of the tongue: and they that love it shall eat the fruit thereof.* (Proverbs 18:21)

The Bible says that *a man's belly shall be satisfied with the fruit of his mouth; and with the increase of his lips shall he be filled.* (Proverbs 18:20) In the school of FAITH, our hearts are filled by what we say, meditate on and think about regularly.

> *Therefore I say unto you,*
> *What things soever ye desire, when ye pray,*
> *believe that ye receive them, and ye shall have them.*
> **Mark 11:24**

The centurion BELIEVED Jesus Christ. The centurion answered and said, *Lord, I am not worthy that thou shouldest come under my roof: but speak the word only, and my servant shall be healed.* (Matthew 8:8)

The woman with the issue of blood believed Jesus Christ. *And a certain woman, which had an issue of blood twelve years, And had suffered many things of many physicians, and had spent all that she had, and was nothing bettered, but rather grew worse, When she had heard of Jesus, came in the press behind, and touched his garment. For she said, If I may touch but his clothes, I shall be whole. And straightway the fountain of her blood was dried up; and she felt in her body that she was healed of that plague.* (Mark 5:25-29)

What we are saying is that faith brings in complete HEALING.

FAITH MAKES WHOLE.

Jesus Christ said to those two blind men, according to your faith—*And when he was come into the house, the blind men came to him: and Jesus saith unto them, Believe ye that I am able to do this? They said unto him, Yea, Lord. Then touched he their eyes, saying, According to your faith be it unto you. And their eyes were opened; and*

Jesus straitly charged them, saying, See that no man know it. (Mathew 9:27-30) As humans, we can pretend in the flesh but GOD looks into the heart. *Jesus Christ see our faith.* (I Samuel 16:7-10) *When Jesus saw their faith, he said unto the sick of the palsy, Son, thy sins be forgiven thee.* (Mark 2:5)

Unless the speaking faith is generated from the heart, it will not be fruitful. If we truly DESIRE anything from GOD, we are admonished to prepare our heart. We cannot be thinking evil thoughts—yet we want faith to work in our favor. We cannot be committing wickedness—yet we expect GOD to be pleased with us. The Bible says in Hebrews 11:6, *But without faith it is impossible to please him: for he that cometh to God must believe that he is, and that he is a rewarder of them that diligently seek him.*

HOW DO YOU GET FAITH?

*Faith comes by hearing,
and hearing by the word of God.*
Romans 10:17

What does this MEAN?

For faith to come by HEARING, and HEARING by the word of GOD, we must constantly be filling our heart and mind with the word of GOD. We must always be optimistic, regardless of the prevailing circumstances. We must therefore put GOD in all we do daily. *For it is God which worketh in you both to will and to do of his good pleasure.* (Philippians 2:13) We all have FAITH inside of our heart to a degree. *According as God hath dealt to every man the measure of faith.* (Romans12:3) Unless we operate by faith, GOD is not pleased with us in life as HIS PEOPLE.

Everyone is given faith. But just like a baby has to learn to speak by hearing his parents, we also have to learn to believe and trust in God by hearing His word. Paul asked the Galatians, who were being bewitched by false Apostles, *"Received you the Spirit by the works of the law or by the hearing of the faith?"* (Galatians 3:2)

The answer is by the hearing of the faith. By hearing God's language of faith. Through the word of God, we receive faith and His Holy Spirit. He also asked them, *"He therefore that ministereth to you in the Spirit, and worketh miracles among you, doeth he it by the works of the law, or by the hearing of the faith?"* (Galatians 3:5) Jesus did His miracles when he heard His believer's faith.

When you are operating in faith, God hears you and does miracles on your behalf. *And when Jesus departed thence, two blind men followed Him, crying, and saying, Thou Son of David, have mercy on us. And when He was come into the house, the blind men came to Him: and Jesus saith unto them, Believe ye that I am able to do this? They said unto Him, Yea, Lord. Then touched He their eyes, saying, According to your faith be it unto you. And their eyes were opened; and Jesus charged them, saying, See that no man know it.* (Matthew 9:27-30)

Lastly, faith is a love language because it worketh by love.

WHAT IS THE FRUIT OF FAITH?

*A man's belly shall be satisfied with
the fruit of his mouth; and with
the increase of his lips shall he be filled.*
Proverbs 18:20

FAITH, as far as I know, never returns void. Every time we get anything accomplished in life, it is by the help of GOD through our faith in Christ Jesus. *And he said unto him, Arise, go thy way: thy faith hath made thee whole.* (Luke 17:19) *Then touched he their eyes, saying, According to your faith be it unto you.* (Matthew 9:29) Faith puts us all in the relevant position with GOD for the manifestation of our expected blessing. When Abraham believed God, it was accounted to him for righteousness. When we belief in the Lord Jesus Christ we receive the gift of salvation and eternal life. *For by grace are ye saved through faith; and that not of yourselves: it is the gift of God.* (Ephesians 2:8; also see John 3:16)

If we have faith as a grain of mustard seed, we move mountains. We overcome our life challenges. God is seeking for FAITHFUL people whom He will bless ABUNDANTLY. The Bible says, "Without faith it is impossible to please God." Whenever we exercise our faith, we prove our submission and loyalty unto God. Oftentimes, we take for granted the things we do by faith. For example, we eat in a restaurant by faith. If there is no faith, we will think twice before ordering for our food. Think about it. How do you believe that this food was cooked right? How do you believe that there is no poison inside of the meal you ordered? Even when we travel on the road or in airplanes, in the air is there not faith? How do you trust that the pilot will get you to your destination? The Bible says, *"And he that doubteth is damned if he eat, because he eateth not of faith: for whatsoever is not of faith is sin."* (Romans 14:23)

THE LAWS OF SPEAKING IN FAITH

...and calleth those things which be not as though they were.
Romans 4:17

In the school of faith, there is no alternative for a wrong negative word. To SPEAK IN FAITH is to enforce the laws of faith. *The law of the speaking faith therefore is an obligation. The law of speaking in faith is a mystery that operates on the flat form of speaking the right word, the seasoned word, the positive word and the desired word.* Most of us are not BOLD enough to truly ask God for what we desire in faith and in prayers.

The Bible says whatsoever we desire when we pray, we should BELIEVE THAT WE RECEIVE THEM AND WE SHALL HAVE THEM. Among the laws of speaking in faith is the law of acting in faith, trust, hope, obeying the Holy Spirit and the law of never confessing a negative word.

HOW DO YOU SPEAK IN FAITH & EXPECT THE MANIFESTATION?

But the manifestation of the Spirit is given to every man to profit withal
1 Corinthians 12:7

Manipulation is a device of the enemy to buffet you.

As a HOLY SPIRIT FILLED BELIEVER, we must be positive in all things. **Every time you are afraid, you have already lost. Speaking with boldness and authority is the key to all manifestation.** *And for me, that utterance may be given unto me, that I may open my mouth boldly, to make known the mystery of the gospel.* (Ephesians 6:19) We cannot win and overcome in life without BOLD DECLARATION IN ALL ASPECTS OF LIFE.

HINDERANCE AGAINST PROVOKING THE MYSTERIES OF FAITH

BITTERNESS

Looking diligently lest any man fail of the grace of God; lest any root of bitterness springing up trouble you, and thereby many be defiled.
Hebrews 12:15

As long as we are bitter in our heart, we cannot speak THE RIGHT WORD. Although **negative words frustrates our lives and circumstances, positive words have the power to prevail, reproduce and manifest in life.** A great man once said, "Whenever you are depressed, you are living in the past. Whenever you are anxious, you are living in the future. But whenever you are at peace, you are living in the present."

The JOY OF THE LORD is the cure for all bitterness in life. *Neither be ye sorry; for the joy of the Lord is your strength.* (Nehemiah 8:10) The joy of the Lord is the platform for all right, faithful declarations. *The spirit of a man will sustain his infirmity; but a wounded spirit who can bear?* (Proverbs 18:14) I admonish you therefore to go after JOY & HAPPINESS in your life. If things must change for you in your lifetime, you must create a conducive atmosphere for the manifestation of the PRESENCE and POWER of GOD. *A merry heart doeth good like a medicine: but a broken spirit drieth the bones.* (Proverbs 17:22)

INIQUITY

But your iniquities have separated between you and your God, and your sins have hid his face from you, that he will not hear.
Isaiah 59:2

Iniquity is the repeating of the sin that easily besets us over and over. As far as I remember, only dogs return to its vomit. GOD has promised us in Jeremiah 31:34, *"For I will forgive their iniquity, and I will remember their sin no more."* Acquaint now thyself with him, and be at peace: thereby good shall come unto thee. Receive, I pray thee, the law from his mouth, and lay up his words in thine heart. If thou return to the Almighty, thou shalt be built up, thou shalt put away iniquity far from thy tabernacles. Then shalt thou layup gold as dust, and the gold of Ophir as the stones of the brooks. (Job 22:21-24) As long as there is sin in our lives, our grammar cannot move GOD. Only RIGHTEOUSNESS moves the HAND & MIND of GOD. He *"hearth not sinners."* (John 9:31)

UN-FORGIVENESS

Un-forgiveness is a device of the devil to destroy faith and the works of faith in us. We easily ask for forgiveness from others, while we all hold others in contempt against the wrong they did to us. **As long as we live and operate in unforgiveness, the power of the speaking faith will be frustrated in our lives.** *For if ye forgive men their trespasses, your heavenly Father will also forgive you: But if ye forgive not men their trespasses, neither will your Father forgive your trespasses. Jeremiah31:34… for I will forgive their iniquity, and I will remember their sin no more.* (Matthew 6:14-15)

REGRET

As I noted earlier, a great man once said,

"When you are depressed, you are living in the past. When you are anxious, you are living in the future. But when you are at PEACE, you are living in the present." *Remember ye not the former things, neither consider the things of old. Behold, I will do a new thing; now it shall spring forth; shall ye not know it? I will even make a way in the wilderness, and rivers in the desert.* (Isaiah 43:18-19) Living in regret drives away the presence of the Holy Spirit. In this race of life, you cannot accomplish nor achieve anything tangible as long as you keep memorizing your shortcomings, past failures, lost moments and lost money. ***Regret is an obstacle to speaking in faith. Every time you operate in regret, you hinder new things from coming into your life.***

ACCESS TO RECIEVE THE PERSON OF THE HOLY SPIRIT

1) BE BORN AGAIN: In these evil days full of terror, it is easy to tell when the un-believer is going through trials and tribulations. As long as you are not a born again Christian all you will get is "sorriooo" and a mere word of comfort—"It is well with you." Of course you know it shall not be well with you. We established earlier that the Holy Spirit does not lead sinners. The Spirit of the Lord comes afresh and becomes a reality once you confess Jesus Christ as your Lord and savior. *Jesus answered and said unto him, Verily, verily, I say unto thee, Except a man be born again, he cannot see the kingdom of*

God. Nicodemus saith unto him, How can a man be born when he is old? can he enter the second time into his mother's womb, and be born? Jesus answered, Verily, verily, I say unto thee, Except a man be born of water and of the Spirit, he cannot enter into the kingdom of God. That which is born of the flesh is flesh; and that which is born of the Spirit is spirit. Marvel not that I said unto thee, Ye must be born again. The wind bloweth where it listeth, and thou hearest the sound thereof, but canst not tell whence it cometh, and whither it goeth: so is every one that is born of the Spirit. (John 3:3-8) Until you confess and acknowledge the Lord Jesus as your savior, you will forever be subdued with trials and tribulations. Eternity is real, therefore if you are not a born again Christian, do so quickly before concluding this Holy Spirit revealed manual.

2) THE FEAR OF GOD: You must develop the consciousness of the fear of God in your heart if you desire to overcome trials and tribulations. As long as you fear God, the help of the Holy Spirit is on the way. The Lord made it clear it shall be well with the righteous, but it shall not be well with the wicked. *Though a sinner do evil an hundred times, and his days be prolonged, yet surely I know that it shall be well with them that fear God, which fear before him: But it shall not be well with the wicked, neither shall he prolong his days, which are as a shadow; because he feareth not before God.* (Ecclesiastes 8:12-13) The Holy Spirit will choose you, to teach you all things once you embrace the fear of God in your life. *What man is he that feareth the Lord? him shall he teach in the way that he shall choose.* (Psalm 25:12)

3) RIGHTEOUS LIFESTYLE: As long as you practice a righteous lifestyle, you will forever enjoy the presence of the Holy Spirit. *Little children, let no man deceive you: he that doeth righteousness is righteous, even as he is righteous.* (1 John 3:7) *And the work of righteousness shall be peace; and the effect of righteousness quietness and assurance forever.* (Isaiah 32:17) Righteousness is the access key to provoke the presence of the Holy Spirit.

4) INTEGRITY: In my own simplified words, the spirit of integrity is the truth. The Holy Spirit is the spirit of truth, therefore the Holy Spirit enjoys everyone who speaks and carries the mantle of the truth in their life. In this race of life, integrity is the access key to provoke the person of the Holy Spirit. *The integrity of the upright shall guide them.* (Proverbs 11:3)

5) AGREEMENT: The Bible asks, *"Can two walk together unless they be agreed?"* (Amos 3:3) Can two walk together, except they be agreed? Agreement is the access gateway for the person of the Holy Spirit. vs19-20 *But if he will not hear thee, then take with thee one or two more, that in the mouth of two or three witnesses every word may be established.* (Matthew 18:16) *Verily I say unto you, Whatsoever ye shall bind on earth shall be bound in heaven: and whatsoever ye shall loose on earth shall be loosed in heaven. Again I say unto you, That if two of you shall agree on earth as touching any thing that they shall ask, it shall be done for them of my Father which is in heaven. For where two or three are gathered together in my name, there am I in* *the midst of them.* (Matthew 18:18-20)

6) THE RIGHT WORDS: Every time you speak the right word, the Holy Spirit comes into your life. Job 6:25 declares, *"How forcible are right words!"* Jesus said there is no idle word in the kingdom. Every time you speak, your words are judged by the angels of the living God. *Suffer not thy mouth to cause thy flesh to sin; neither say thou before the angel, that it was an error: wherefore should God be angry at thy voice, and destroy the work of thine hands?* (Ecclesiastes 5:6) The right words will bring you out of captivity, the right word will provoke the Holy Spirit to come to your rescue.

7) SOUL WINNING: We must win souls for the kingdom of God. Faith, the Bible says, works by love. *For God so loved the world that he gave...* (John 3:16) **Soul winning for the kingdom of God proves our loyalty and obedience to the word of God. Faith works easily for every soul winner because God is pleased with them.**

And Jesus came and spake unto them, saying,
All power is given unto me in heaven and in earth.
Go ye therefore, and teach all nations, baptizing them in
the name of the Father, and of the Son, and of the Holy
Ghost: Teaching them to observe all things whatsoever
I have commanded you: and, lo, I am with you always,
even unto the end of the world. Amen.
Matthew 28:18-20

8) OBEDIENCE: As long as you are walking in disobedience, you will never experience the manifestation of the Holy Spirit. Remember he is the seal of redemption. *In whom ye also trusted, after that ye heard the word of truth, the gospel of your salvation: in whom also after that ye believed, ye were sealed with that holy Spirit of promise.* (Ephesians 1:13) *Obey them that have the rule over you, and submit yourselves: for they watch for your souls, as they that must give account, that they may do it with joy, and not with grief: for that is unprofitable for you. (*Hebrews 13:17)

9) PRAY IN THE SPIRIT: Faith cannot manifest unless we pray in the Holy Spirit. *But ye, beloved, building up yourselves on your most holy faith, praying in the Holy Ghost.* (Jude 1:20)

Let's examine these 12 laws I found in Hebrews 11

THE LAW OF EXISTENCE

We must believe that GOD is active and alive in all our affairs in life.

THE LAW OF JUST PROVIDENCE

We must believe that God rewards those who work hard in life and those who diligently seek God.

THE LAW OF BELIEVING THE UNSEEN
(MIRACLES & SUPERNATURAL)

We must believe God for, and in, the supernatural. You will frustrate the manifestation of your spoken word with unbelief.

THE LAW OF TRUST

We must believe and trust God on divine arrangement. *And we know that all things work together for good to them that love God, to them who are the called according to his purpose.* (Romans 8:28)

THE LAW OF ENDURANCE

We will frustrate the will, purpopse and plan of God over our lives with impatience. We must examplify our life, after men like father Abraham in the Bible who waited and endured for 100 years before getting a son (Isaac). *Cast not away therefore your confidence, which hath great recompence of reward. For ye have need of patience, that, after ye have done the will of God, ye might receive the promise.* (Hebrews 10:35-36)

THE LAW OF ASSURED CONVICTION

We must transfer all our worries and challenges into the ALMIGHTY GOD. Whenever God takes over any challenge of life, the battle becomes over.

THE LAW OF BELIEVING THE IMPOSSIBLE

We must believe God for all things. we must apply faith to impossible situation. *Now the Lord had said unto Abram, Get thee out of thy country, and from thy kindred, and from thy father's house, unto a land that I will shew thee: And I will make of thee a great nation, and I will bless thee, and make thy name great; and thou shalt be a blessing: And I will bless them that bless thee, and curse him that curseth thee: and in thee shall all families of the earth be blessed. So Abram departed, as the Lord had spoken unto him; and Lot went with him: and Abram was seventy and five years old when he departed out of Haran.* (Genesis 12:1-4)

THE LAW OF BELIEF & CONFIDENCE

We must totally depend on and believe in God. We must be convicted by the Holy Spirit. Our trust must be established in all we do in life. And this is the confidence that we have in Him that, if we ask anything according to His will, He heareth us. *And if we know that he hear us, whatsoever we ask, we know that we have the petitions that we desired of him.* (1 John 5:15) Again talking about Abraham, the Bible says, *"And he believed in the Lord; and he counted it to him for righteousness."* (Genesis 15:6, James 2:23)

THE LAW OF AMBITION FOR ETERNITY

Faith admonishes us to work out our own salvation with fear and trembling. We must be conscious of our life now—and the life after death. Salvation came by love. (John 3:16) For GOD so loved, he gave… (John 3:16) Remember Galatians 5:6—*Faith works by love. Faith seeks the city that is to come.*

THE LAW OF ALL POSSIBILITY

We must be convinced that all things are possible with God. That is the answer to all of life's prevailing problems. *And Jesus looking upon them saith; With men it is impossible, but not with God: for with God all things are possible.* (Mark 10:27) *For with God nothing shall be impossible.* (Luke 1:37)

THE LAW OF RENUNCIATION

Faith dominates and overrides whatsoever that is not faith. Faith establishes our roots in the seed of Abraham and our engrafting in Christ Jesus. *He staggered not at the promise of God through unbelief; but was strong in faith, giving glory to God; And being fully persuaded that, what he had promised, he was able also to perform.* (Romans 4:20-21) *And he that doubteth is damned if he eat, because he eateth not of faith: **for whatsoever is not of faith is sin.*** (Romans 14:23)

THE LAW OF CONQUEST

Faith never accepts defeat, in all things. If you truly have faith, it must show, there must be proof. Y*ea, a man may say, Thou hast faith, and I have works: shew me thy faith without thy works, and I will shew thee my faith by my works.* (James 2:18) FAITH resists persecution and testifying to the glory of God. It took Queen Esther's faith to say, "if I perish, I perish." Faith as simply as it can be defined, does not succumb to prevailing circumstances.

WAYS IN WHICH THE HOLY SPIRIT LEADS & DIRECTS US

AUDIBLE VOICE: The Holy Spirit speaks to us. The Bible says in Acts 10:19, *"while Peter thought on the vision the Holy Spirit said unto him, Behold three men seek thee.* And then there was this—*As they ministered to the Lord, and fasted, the Holy Ghost said, Separate me Barnabas and Saul for the work whereunto I have called them. If you are not in the Spirit you can get into the spirit by singing a heavenly song unto the Holy Spirit.* (Acts 13:2) This I called melody.

MELODY: Every time you sing unto the Lord, you are bound to hear His voice in a song or melody—through singing sweet songs late at night or early in the morning. *And the Lord shall cause his glorious voice to be heard,* *and shall shew the lighting down of his arm, with the indignation of his anger, and with the flame of a devouring fire, with scattering, and tempest, and hailstones. For through the voice of the Lord shall the Assyrian be beaten down, which smote with a rod.* (Isaiah 30:29) *For the Lord shall comfort Zion: he will comfort all her waste places; and he will make her wilderness like Eden, and her desert like the garden of the Lord; joy and gladness shall be found therein, thanksgiving, and the voice of melody.* (Isaiah 51:3) You provoke the Holy Spirit into action once you lift up spiritual songs to minister to the Spirit. *While Peter yet spake these words, the Holy Ghost fell on all them which heard the word.* (Acts 10:44)

THROUGH THY WORD: Every life question and answer is in the Bible. Abbreviated B.I.B.L.E means:

B-------- Basic
I------------------Instruction
B---------------------------------Before
L---------------------------------------Leaving
E --Earth

The word of God is the only life manual relevant and applicable to all ages, for all men and for all times. The Bible is the most referenced book for businesses, government establishments, marriage institutions and all aspects of life. *Thy word is a lamp unto my feet, and a light unto my path.* (Psalms 119:105)

OVERCOMING BY THE HELP OF THE HOLY SPIRIT

These things I have spoken unto you, that in me ye might have peace. In the world ye shall have tribulation: but be of good cheer; I have overcome the world.
John 16:33

Although we live and operate in a physical kingdom, where trial and temptation is bound to come to pass in our lifetime, God gave us the precious Holy Spirit to strengthen and minister to us in time of trouble. As long as you live, temptation and trial will come. But thank God for victory. *There hath no temptation taken you but such as is common to man: but God is faithful, who will not suffer you to be tempted above that ye are able; but will with the temptation also make a way to escape, that ye may be able to bear it.* (1 Corinthians 10:13)

My mentor once said that life is in phases, while men are in seizes. In my view, every level in life comes with a challenge. Just like my mentor used to say, there is no mountain anywhere in the world—your present mountain is your ignorance. Information is the relevant access code to break through to that level. The access key here is relevant information that is life transforming.

The accomplished milestone in your life is the result of the available information to your reach. Ask the Holy Spirit to make you access relevant information to overcome any present challenge, trial and tribulation. Engage the Holy Spirit as your very present help in all times—not only in times of trouble. At every level of your life there is always a challenge, an obstacle to conquer. It has been proven that as long as you have the companionship of the Holy Spirit, you will overcome any prevailing challenge.

> *I will lift up mine eyes unto the hills,*
> *from whence cometh my help.*
> *My help cometh from the Lord,*
> *which made heaven and earth.*
> **Psalms 121:1-2**

As long as you take the Holy Spirit serious in your life, God will also take you serious. Jesus made it clear to us all in John 16:33—*These things I have spoken unto you, that in me ye might have peace. In the world ye shall have tribulation: but be of good cheer; I have overcome the world.* That you are now a born again, fire baptized, speaking in tongues and in the Holy Ghost does not exempt you from experiencing life challenges.

As a believer you have the privilege to acquaint your life with the help of the Holy Spirit. (See John 14:18, 26) You have the accreditation as a spiritual law enforcement officer to evict demons far away from your life. You have the last weapon—the blood of Jesus—to overcome Satan and his cohorts. More also have the power of attorney in the Name of Jesus. *And whatsoever ye shall ask in my name, that will I do, that the Father may be glorified in the Son. If ye shall ask any thing in my name,*

I will do it. (John 14:13-14)

The summary of the trials and tribulations of life is your ability to understand life from a spiritual perspective. Life will not favor you until you are ready to put up a fight. *Fight the good fight of faith, lay hold on eternal life, whereunto thou art also called, and hast professed a good profession before many witnesses.* (1 Timothy 6:12)

"What you do not want, you don't watch."

"What you do not resist has power to remain."

"What you do not confront, you cannot conquer."

These quotes are the solution to every challenge you will ever encounter in life. Most of our shortcomings are related to our inability to confront challenging situations.

Prerequisites to overcome trials & tribulations

1) BE BORN AGAIN: In these evil days full of terror, it is easy to tell when the un-believer is going through trials and tribulations. As long as you are not a born again Christian all you will get is "sorriooo" and a mere word of comfort—"It is well with you." Of course you know it shall not be well with you. We established earlier that the Holy Spirit does not lead sinners. The Spirit of the Lord comes afresh and becomes a reality once you confess Jesus Christ as your Lord and savior. *Jesus answered and said unto him, Verily, verily, I say unto thee,*

Except a man be born again, he cannot see the kingdom of God. Nicodemus saith unto him, How can a man be born when he is old? can he enter the second time into his mother's womb, and be born? Jesus answered, Verily, verily, I say unto thee, Except a man be born of water and of the Spirit, he cannot enter into the kingdom of God. That which is born of the flesh is flesh; and that which is born of the Spirit is spirit. Marvel not that I said unto thee, Ye must be born again. The wind bloweth where it listeth, and thou hearest the sound thereof, but canst not tell whence it cometh, and whither it goeth: so is every one that is born of the Spirit. (John 3:3-8) Until you confess and acknowledge the Lord Jesus as your savior, you will forever be subdued with trials and tribulations. Eternity is real, therefore if you are not a born again Christian, do so quickly before concluding this Holy Spirit revealed manual.

2) THE FEAR OF GOD: You must develop the consciousness of the fear of God in your heart if you desire to overcome trials and tribulations. As long as you fear God, the help of the Holy Spirit is on the way. The Lord made it clear it shall be well with the righteous, but it shall not be well with the wicked. *Though a sinner do evil an hundred times, and his days be prolonged, yet surely I know that it shall be well with them that fear God, which fear before him: But it shall not be well with the wicked, neither shall he prolong his days, which are as a shadow; because he feareth not before God.* (Ecclesiastes 8:12-13) The Holy Spirit will choose you, to teach you all things once you embrace the fear of God in your life. *What man is he* *that feareth the Lord? him shall he teach in the way that he shall choose.* (Psalms 25:12)

3) BOLDNESS: Always be bold to go before God and ask him for help and demand the presence of the Holy Spirit. *Let us therefore come boldly unto the throne of grace that we may obtain mercy, and find grace to help in time of need.* (Hebrews 4:16) All of us believers have the accreditation by the blood of Jesus to exercise boldness in all area of our lives. Until you put out boldness, your prevailing obstacles have power to remain. I summon you to gather boldness and allow the Holy Spirit to destroy those hindering obstacles in your life, in the Name of Jesus. *And when they had prayed, the place was shaken where they were assembled together; and they were all filled with the Holy Ghost, and they spake the word of God with boldness.* (Acts 14:31)

4) AUTHORITY: Oftentimes we forget who is in charge. Jesus fulfilled his precious promise to send the Holy Spirit to help us here on Earth. *Nevertheless I tell you the truth; It is expedient for you that I go away: for if I go not away, the Comforter will not come unto you; but if I depart, I will send him unto you.* (John 16:7) In my opinion, the Holy Spirit delivers the necessary authority to confront prevailing and challenging obstacles. Therefore, gather authority and destroy that prevailing circumstance in your life. *Then he called his twelve disciples together, and gave them power and authority over all devils, and to cure diseases.* (Luke 9:1)

5) HAVE FAITH IN GOD: It takes faith to overcome trials and tribulations in life. *But without faith it is impossible to please him: for he that cometh to God must believe that he is, and that he is a rewarder of them that diligently seek him.* (Hebrews 11:6) The reason God will grant you victory is because you pleased Him. Remember Proverbs 16:7—*When a man's ways please the Lord, he maketh even his enemies to be at peace with him.*

6) BE IN AGREEMENT WITH THE HOLY SPIRIT: The Holy Spirit will leave you alone to solve your problem when you walk in disagreement. As long as you are in disagreement, you are on your own. Come into agreement today with the Holy Spirit and let him take over all your troubles and hardship. *Can two walk together, except they be agreed?* (Amos 3:3)

7) DEVELOP A WINNING MENTALITY: To develop a winning mentality means to go all out for victory by all righteous means. A great man once said you cannot climb the ladder of success dressed in the costume of failure. Most winners do not quit—remember, quitters do not win. To overcome your present trials and tribulations means you must confront all of life's challenging issues as they come into your life. The Bible says in John 16:33, *"These things I have spoken unto you, that in me ye might have peace. In the world ye shall have tribulation: but be of good cheer; I have overcome the world."*

8) ENDURANCE: No matter the trial and level of tribulation, never give up in your quest to overcome your present trials. As long as you can endure to the end, the sky is your limit. *And ye shall be hated of all men for my name's sake: but he that endureth to the end shall be saved.* (Matthew 10:22)

9) BE MEEK: Even if you are naturally an arrogant and proud person, common sense tells you that in times of trial and tribulation you should humble yourself and allow the Holy Spirit to take over the prevailing challenges facing you. *The meek will he guide in judgment: and the meek will he teach his way.* (Psalms 25:9) As far as it is the Holy Spirit, your best efforts are His—the Holy Spirit's—beginning.

10) WALK IN LOVE: Exemplify your life like the life of Job. In the midst of great destruction, Job said, "Though he slay me, yet will I trust in him: but I will maintain mine own ways before him." You can lose all, but don't lose your covenant LOVE for God and His Kingdom. *But he knoweth the way that I take: when he hath tried me, I shall come forth as gold.* (Job 23:10) Job's victory came as a result of His LOVE for GOD and the Kingdom of GOD.

PRAYER POINTS TO DOMINATE REMOTE CONTROL FORCES

1) Father Lord, deliver me from this present trial, in the Name of Jesus.

2) Almighty Father, break me out of this present obscurity, in the Name of Jesus.

3) Holy Spirit, help me to overcome this trial, in Jesus Name.

4) Holy Spirit, speak to me, in the Name of Jesus.

5) Holy Spirit, minister to my subconscious spirit, in the Name of Jesus.

6) Fire of God, burn down every mountain of difficulty, in the Name of Jesus.

7) Holy Ghost, baptize me with your fire, in the Name of Jesus.

8) Holy Spirit, go before me and favor me in this present challenge, in the Name of Jesus.

9) Spirit of God, grant me liberty and freedom by the fire of the Holy Spirit, in the Name of Jesus.

10) Father Lord, intervene on my behalf, in the Name of Jesus.

11) Ancient of day, liberate me this season, in the Name of Jesus.

12) Immortal redeemer, bring me higher above these prevailing changes.

13) Lord God, turn this present obstacale into my miracle, in the Name of Jesus.

14) Fire of God, break down these obstacles for me, in the Name of Jesus.

15) Holy Spirit, favor me in, Jesus Name.

16) Holy Spirit. release me from this challenge, in the Name of Jesus.

17) Holy Spirit, become my compionion, in Jesus Name.

18) Holy Spirit, represent me in this matter.

19) Holy Spirit, elevant me beyond my own immagination, in the Name of Jesus.

20) Holy Spirit, do not allow my enemies to truimph over my life, in the Name of Jesus.

21) Fire of God, protect me, in the Name of Jesus.

22) Fire of God, destroy my enemies, in the Name of Jesus.

23) Fire of God, build a wall around me, in the Name of Jesus.

24) Fire of God, expose my enemies, in the Name of Jesus.

25) Fire of God, prove yourself, in the Name of Jesus.

26) Holy Spirit, represent me in jesus name.

27) Holy Spirit, release your boldnes into my life.

28) Holy Spirit, grant me signs and wonders.

29) Holy Spirit, make me a living wonder in my lifetime.

30) Holy Spirit, turn my life around, in the Name of Jesus.

31) Holy Spirit, I will not remain at this level, in the Name of Jesus.

32) Spirit of God, lift me higher, in the mighty Name of Jesus.

33) Angels of God, minister unto me, in the Name of Jesus.

34) Hand of God, separate me this season, in the Name of Jesus.

CONCLUSION

And calleth those things
which be not as though they were.
Romans 4:17

FAITH is so POWERFUL that it DOMINATES & RULES our lives. In our lifetime we should never take for granted the things faith will accomplish for us, especially with our glorious destinies. Faith is the recovery link, the building block and the solid foundation for all great destinies.

Yea, a man may say, Thou hast faith, and I have works:
shew me thy faith without thy works, and I will shew
thee my faith by my works.
James 2:18

We must be ***hard working people***, for all faith proclamation without hard work is unfruitful and wrong. God promised to bless us, but we must engage our mind soul, spirit and body in working. *Whatsoever thy hand findeth to do, do it with thy might.* (Ecclesiastes 9:10) *And whatsoever he doeth shall prosper.* (Psalms 1:3)

For as the body without the spirit is dead,
so faith without works is dead also.
James 2:26

We must always be conscious of the word we speak at any time. There is POWER IN SPEAKING THE RIGHT WORD to under any prevailing circumstance.

Let no corrupt communication proceed out of your mouth, but that which is good to the use of edifying, that it may minister grace unto the hearers.
Ephesians 4:29

We must all obey the Holy Spirit by what we say at any time of the day. Most of us have neglected the person of the Holy Spirit. Remember, even Jesus Christ needed the help of the Holy Spirit. *How God anointed Jesus of Nazareth with the Holy Ghost and with power: who went about doing good, and healing all that were oppressed of the devil; for God was with him.* (Acts 10:38)

Without contradiction, without the person of the Holy Spirit, we are helpless against the wiles and schemes of the devil. I will not leave you comfortless: I will come to you. But the Comforter, which is the Holy Ghost, whom the Father will send in my name, he shall teach you all things, and bring all things to your remembrance, whatsoever I have said unto you. We must develop a ***prayer lifstyle*** and a ***lifestyle of righteousness***.

That which is born of the flesh is flesh; and that which is born of the Spirit is spirit. (John 3:6)

As a true believer, we must be born of theSpirit of God. We must live by the Spirit of God.

Let us hear the conclusion of the whole matter:
Fear God, and keep his commandments:
for this is the whole duty of man.
For God shall bring every work into judgment,
with every secret thing,
whether it be good, or whether it be evil.
Ecclesiastes 12:13-14

The POWER OF GOD is provoked only when you FEAR GOD and keep His commandments. The Bible says in Ecclesiastes 12:14—F*or God shall bring every work into judgment, with every secret thing, whether it be good, or whether it be evil.* If you are a born again Christian, we like to encourage you in your Christian life. If you are not a born again Christian, we can help you here receive genuine salvation.

Therefore if any man be in Christ,
he is a new creature: old things are passed away;
behold, all things are become new.
2 Corinthians 5:17

WHAT MUST I DO TO DETERMINE MY DIVINE VISITATION?

To determine divine visitation you must be born again! The word says as many as received Him, to them gave He power to become the sons of God. Even to them that believe on His name.

To qualify for divine visitation, do the following sincerly:

1) Acknowledge that you are a sinner and that He died for you. (Romans 3:23)

2) Repent of your sins. (Acts 3:19, Luke 13:5, 2 Peter 3:9)

3) Believe in your heart that Jesus died for your sin.(Romans 10:10)

4) Confess Jesus as the Lord over your life. (Romans 10:10, Acts 2:21)

NOW REPEAT THIS PRAYER AFTER ME:
Say Lord Jesus, I accept you today, as my Lord and my savior, forgive me of my sins wash me with your blood. Right now, I believe, I am sanctified, I am saved, I am free, I am free from the power of sin to serve the Lord Jesus. Thank you Lord for saving me. Amen.

Congratulations.

YOU ARE NOW A BORN AGAIN CHRISTAIN!

Again, I say to you—congratulations! I adjure you to watch the Spirit of God bear witness with your Spirit confirming His word with signs following. The word says the Spirit itself beareth witness with our spirit, that we are the children of God Join a Bible-believing church or join us on our weekly and Sunday worship services at 343 Sanford Ave., Newark, NJ 07106.

WISDOM KEYS

— Every productive society is a society heading to the top.

—Millions of Nigerians run away from Nigeria. Very few Nigerians stay in Nigeria.

—My decision to return Nigeria is the will of God for my life.

—My shortcoming in America after 18 years is the fact that I've trained me to be wise, to think, reflect and reason appropriately.

—If you train your mind to reason, it will train your hands to earn money.

—It is absurd to use the money of the heathen to build the kingdom of the living God.

—Every ministry reveals its agenda and VISION either at the beginning or at the end.

—Be careful of your life. It is your first ministry.

—The average American mind is conditioned for a continual quest to get new things and discard the old.

—When I considered well, my BMW jeep became my initial deposit for the work of the ministry in Nigeria.

—Money will never fall from any tree or person. Make up your mind to be independent today.

—Everyone is waiting for you to change your mind. Until you change your thinking, nothing changes around you.

—Multiple academic degrees in other disciplines gave me the chance to think and reason.

—Whatever anyone is thinking at any time reveals what is inside of their heart.

—All planned events are the product of meditation.

—Every event is designed for a designated timeline.

—Wisdom is your ability to think, to create and invent.

— If you can think wisely enough, you will come out of debt.

—The distance between you and your success is your innovative and creative ability to think well.

—Success is the result of hard work, commitment, resolve and determined learning from past mistakes and failings.

—If you organize your mind, you have organized your life and destiny.

—There is a thin line between success and failure.

—Wealth is your ability to think, power is your ability to reason and success is your ability to be informed.

—If you can make use of your mind by thinking and reasoning, God will make use of your life and destiny.

—Reflect, reason, think and be Great.

—Famous people are born of woman.

—That you will make it is your intention, that you will survive is your resolve, that you will succeed with changes is your determination, personal efforts and hard work.

—No man was born a failure.

—Lack of vision is the result of failure.

—Working with mental patients encourages and aspire me to be a productive observant and dedicated to my assignment.

—Successful people are not magicians. It is the willpower, combined with hard work and determination and a resolve to succeed, that make them succeed.

—In the unequivocal state of the mind, intention is not a location or a position. It is the state of the mind.

—So many people think that they think.

—The mind is used to think, to reflect and to reason.

—You will remain blind with your eyes open until you can see with your mind by thinking.

—There is no favoritism in accurate and precise calculation.

—Although knowledge is power, information is the key and gateway to a great future.

—It will take the hand of God to move the hand of man.

—With the backing of the great wise God, nothing will disconnect you from your inheritance.

—As long as you have wisdom and understanding of God, Satan and evil cannot manipulate your life and destiny.

CHAPTER 4
PRAYER OF SALVATION

I am glad you have read this book all the way from the beginning to this point. All I have said from the beginning will remain a mystery until you commit it into practice.

And before you do so, I want you, if you have not given your life to Jesus yet, to do so now. Give your life to Christ. I want you to know the truth! The truth is that Jesus died for your sins. And because He died, you must be alive and prosperous.

What must I do to determine my divine visitation?

To determine divine visitation, you must be born again! The word says as many as received Him, to them gave He power to become the sons of God. Even to them that believe on His name.

To qualify for divine visitation, do the following sincerely:

1) Acknowledge that you are a sinner and that He died for you. (Romans 3:23)

2) Repent of your sins. (Acts 3:19, Luke 13:5, 2 Peter 3:9)

3) Believe in your heart that Jesus died for your sin.
(Romans 10:10)

4) Confess Jesus as the Lord over your life.
(Romans 10:10, Acts 2:21)

> ***NOW REPEAT THIS PRAYER AFTER ME:***
> *Say Lord Jesus, I accept you today,*
> *as my Lord and my savior, forgive me of my sins*
> *wash me with your blood. Right now, I believe,*
> *I am sanctified, I am save, I am free, I am free*
> *from the power of sin to serve the Lord Jesus.*
> *Thank you Lord for saving me. Amen.*

Congratulations.

YOU ARE NOW A BORN AGAIN CHRISTAIN!

Again, I say to you—congratulations!

I adjure you to watch the Spirit of God bear witness with your Spirit confirming His word with signs following. The word says the Spirit itself beareth witness with our spirit, that we are the children of God.

MIRACLE CARE OUTREACH

*"...But that the members should have
the same care one for another"*
1 Corinthians 12:25

We are all members of the body of Christ. Jesus commanded us to love our neighbor as ourselves. This includes caring for one another as a member of one body. True love is expressed in caring and giving. The word says, for God so Love He gave....

Reach out to someone in need of Jesus. Help someone in crisis find Christ. Look out and prove your love to Jesus by caring and inviting your friends and associates to find Jesus the Healer.

Invite your friends to our Home Care Cell Fellowship (Miracle Chapel Intl. Satellite Fellowship). We're in the U.S. at 33 Schley Street, Newark, New Jersey 07112. Home Care Cell Fellowship Group meets every Tuesday at 6:00pm-7:00pm.

If you are in Nigeria—MIRACLE OF GOD MINISTRIES, aka "MIRACLE CHAPEL INTL." Mpama–Egbu-Owerri Imo state Nigeria.

LIFE IS NOT ALL ABOUT DURATION, BUT IT'S ALL ABOUT DONATION

What does this statement mean?

Life consists not in accumulation of material wealth. (Luke 12:15) But it's all about liberality...i.e., what you can give and share with others. (Proverbs 11:25) When you live for others, you live forever—because you outlive your generation by the legacy you leave behind after you depart into glory to be with the Lord. But when you live for yourself, when you are reduced to SELF—you are easily forgotten when you die and depart in glory.

Permit me to admonish you today to live your life to be a blessing to a soul connected to you today. I want you to know that so many souls are connected and looking up to you, and through you so many souls will be saved and rescued from destruction. Will you disciple someone today to find Jesus Christ?

As a genuine Christian, it is your duty to evangelize Jesus Christ to all you meet on your way. Jesus is still in the healing business—Jesus is still doing miracles, from time of old to now. Therefore, tell someone about Jesus Christ today, disciple and bring them to Church. *Philip findeth Nathanael...* (John 1:45)

Please prove the sincerity of your love for God today, please become a soul winner. The dignity of your Christianity is hidden in your boldness to proclaim and evangelize Jesus Christ to all you meet on your way. There is a question mark on the integrity of your Christianity until you become a life soul winner. Invite someone to join us worship the Lord Jesus this coming Sunday.

MIRACLE OF GOD MINISTRIES
PILLARS OF THE COMMISSION

We Believe, Preach and Practice the following:

1) We believe and preach Salvation to every living human being.

2) We believe and preach Repentance and Forgiveness of sins.

3) We believe and preach the baptism of the Holy Spirit and Spiritual gifts.

4) We believe and teach Prosperity.

5) We believe and preach Divine Healing and Miracles—Signs and Wonder.

6) We believe and preach Faith.

7) We believe and proclaim the Power of God (Supernatural).

8) We believe and proclaim Praise and Worship to God.

9) We believe and preach Wisdom.

10) We believe and preach Holiness (Consecration).

11) We believe and preach Vision.

12) We believe and teach the Word of God.

13) We believe and teach Success.

14) We believe and practice Prayer.

15) We believe and teach Deliverance.

These 15 stones form the Pillars of Our Commission.

MY HEARTFELT PRAYER FOR YOU

It is my burning desire for God to touch you through one of our teaching books or CDs. It also my personal desire for you encounter God for yourself.

Now let me pray for you:

O Lord God! I beseech thee, and through personal prayer intercession today that the Holy Spirit will touch you reading this book and turn you life around.
In the Name of Jesus, I speak faith into your life today.
I come against all oppressive though,
in Jesus Name. Amen.

TIME TO TURN TO GOD

Have you ever asked why are you here? God planted you here to bring to pass his plan—to counsel and plan over your life.

The best of your physical strength and efforts are the beginning of God's grace.

Eternity is real, heaven is sure. Become interested in the heavenly race and book your name in the lamb book of life.

Everything great comes by His grace upon your life. Therefore, turn unto God in supplication—in thanksgiving and in prayer—and God will turn in your favor.

ABOUT THE AUTHOR

Rev. Franklin N. Abazie is the founding and Presiding Pastor of Miracle of God Ministries, with headquarters in Newark, New Jersey USA and a branch church in Owerri-Imo State Nigeria. He is following the footsteps of one of his mentors, the healing evangelist Oral Roberts of the blessed memory. The Lord passed Oral Roberts' healing mantle two days before he went to be with the Lord at age 91 into the hands of healing evangelist Rev. Franklin N. Abazie in a vision.

In all his services, the Power and Presence of God is present to heal all in his audience. Rev. Abazie is an ordained man of God, with a Healing Ministry reviving the healing and miracle ministry of Jesus Christ of Nazareth.

Pastor Franklin N. Abazie, has been called by God with a unique mandate: **"THE MOMENT IS DUE TO IMPACT YOUR WORLD THROUGH THE REVIVAL OF THE HEALING AND MIRACLE MINISTRY OF JESUS CHRIST OF NAZARETH.**

"I AM SENDING YOU TO RESTORE HEALTH UNTO THEE AND I WILL HEAL THEE OF THY WOUNDS, SAID THE LORD OF HOST"

Rev. Abazie is a gifted, ardent teacher of the word of God, who operates also in the office of a Prophet, generating and attracting undeniable signs and wonders, special miracles and healings, with apostolic fireworks of the Holy Ghost. He is the founding and presiding senior Pastor of this fast growing Healing Ministry. He has written over 86 inspirational, healing and transforming books covering almost all aspects of divine healing and life. He is happily married and blessed with children.

BOOKS BY REV. FRANKLIN N. ABAZIE:

1) The Outcome of Faith
2) Understanding the Secret of Prevailing Prayers
3) Commanding Abundance
4) Understanding the Secret of the Man God Uses
5) Activating My Due Season
6) Overcoming Divine Verdicts
7) The Outcome of Divine Wisdom
8) Understanding God's Restoration Mandate
9) Walking In the Victory and Authority of the Truth
10) God's Covenant Exemption
11) Destiny Restoration Pillars
12) Provoking Acceptable Praise
13) Understanding Divine Judgment
14) Activating Angelic Re-enforcement
15) Provoking Un-Merited Favo
16) The Benefits of the Speaking Faith
17) Understanding Divine Arrangement
18) How to Keep Your Healing
19) Understanding the Mysteries of the Speaking Faith
20) Understanding the Mysteries of Prophetic Healing
21) Operating Under the Rules of Creative Healing
22) Understanding the Joy of Breakthrough
23) Understanding the Mystery of Breakthrough
24) Understanding Divine Prosperity
25) Understanding Divine Healing
26) Retaining Your Inheritance
27) Overcoming Confusing Spirit
28) Commanding Angelic Escorts

29) Enforcing Your Inheritance In Christ Jesus
30) Understanding Your Guardian Angels
31) Overcoming the Dominion of Sin
32) Understanding the Voice of God
33) The Outstanding Benefits of the Anointing
34) The Audacity of the Blood of Jesus
35) Walking in the Reality of the Anointing
36) Escaping the Nightmare of Poverty
37) Understanding Your Harvest Season
38) Activating Your Success Buttons
39) Overcoming the Forces of Darkness
40) Overcoming the Devices of the Devil
41) Overcoming Demonic Agents
42) Overcoming the Sorrows of Failure
43) Rejecting the Sorrows of Failure
44) Resisting the Sorrows of Poverty
45) Restoring Broken Marriages
46) Redeeming Your Days
47) The Force of Vision
48) Overcoming the Forces of Ignorance
49) Understanding the Sacrifice of Small Beginning
50) The Might of Small Beginning
51) Understanding the Mysteries of Prophesy
52) Overcoming Dream Nightmares
53) Breaking the Shackles of the Curse of the Law
54) Understanding the Joy of Harvest
55) Wisdom for Signs & Wonders
56) Wisdom for Generational Impact
57) Wisdom for Marriage Stability
58) Understanding the Number of Your Days

59) Enforcing Your Kingdom Rights
60) Escaping the Traps of Immoralities
61) Escaping the Trap of Poverty
62) Accessing Biblical Prosperity
63) Accessing True Riches in Christ
64) Silencing the Voice of the Accuser
65) Overcoming the Forces of Oppositions
66) Quenching the Voice of the Avenger
67) Silencing Demonic Prediction & Projection
68) Silencing Your Mocker
69) Understanding the Power of the Holy Ghost
70) Understanding the Baptism of Power
71) The Mystery of the Blood of Jesus
72) Understanding the Mystery of Sanctification
73) Understanding the Power of Holiness
74) Understanding the Forces of Purity & Righteousness
75) Activating the Forces of Vengeance
76) Appreciating the Mystery of Restoration
77) Overcoming the Projection & Prediction of the Enemy
78) Engaging the Mystery of the Blood
79) Commanding the Power of the Speaking Faith
80) Uprooting the Forces Against Your Rising
81) Overcoming Mere Success Syndrome
82) Understanding Divine Sentence
83) Understanding the Mystery of Praise
84) Understanding the Author of Faith
85) The Mystery of the Finisher of Faith
86) Attracting Supernatural Favor

MIRACLE OF GOD MINISTRIES

NIGERIA CRUSADE 2012

MIRACLE OF GOD MINISTRIES
NIGERIA CRUSADE
2012

MIRACLE OF GOD MINISTRIES
NIGERIA CRUSADE 2012

MIRACLE OF GOD MINISTRIES

NIGERIA CRUSADE

2012

MIRACLE OF GOD MINISTRIES

NIGERIA CRUSADE

2012

www.ingramcontent.com/pod-product-compliance
Lightning Source LLC
Chambersburg PA
CBHW021447080526
44588CB00009B/732